Growing Up

Ella Di Marco

Presentation by *BookLeaf Publishing*

Web: www.bookleafpub.com

E-mail: info@bookleafpub.com

ISBN: 9789357446938

First edition 2022

My Dot

There is a dot,
A tiny dot.
The dot is too small.

I wait to see a flicker.
I wait for good news.
It never comes.

Outside in the cool breeze
The trees still shake in the wind.
A mother calls her child.
The red man still turns green,
I still have to walk.

Home

Out the window I see trees;
So many trees.
I hear the birds.
The birds sing loudly,
Happily.
Welcome us.

The garden is warm.
Cars drawn in chalk on the tiles.
Strawberries attempting to grow.
The smell of jasmine envelops us.

First steps taken
On carpet,
From mum to dad.
Topple over.
In our home.

Standing outside the bathroom.
"You look first."
Bare feet on tiles.
Two pink lines.
We smile.
We cry.
In our home.

We are not ready to leave.
The birds still sing for us,
The jasmine calms us.
Goodbye our home.

In The Garden

Sweaty hands.
Fist full of flowers.
Dinosaur's lunch,
By the steps,
In the sun.

Red ball thrown;
Lost in long grass.
"Dad will mow soon,"
She says, third week in a row.

Dance party.
No music.
We dance anyway.
To the song in our hearts,
Played on trees and flowers;
The birds are backup singers

Airplane!
Quick look.
In the sky
An airplane goes by.
Wave.
Say hi.
An airplane goes by.

Snack time.
"No inside.
Snack nom nom nom."
In the shade.
Sticky hands,
Watermelon lips.
"Cookie?"
"Not today."

Quickening

Are you okay?
How do I know?
Quesy mornings.
Tired afternoons.
Spicy food,
Raspberries and tacos.
But are you okay?

Jeans too small now.
Out of breath.
The smell of eggs,
Gets me out of here.
But are you okay?

Butterfly kisses:
Tap tap tap.
Roll inside.
There you are.
Now I know you're okay.

I sit still and wait,
My hand on my belly.
Anxious,
Worried.
Please don't be like last time.

Tap tap.
There you are.
All is okay.
For now.

The Teddy and the Lamb

A teddy and a lamb.
Hold them close,
Cry into their fur.
They are always there.

I knock on your door,
Make sure you're okay.
"It isn't fair," you say,
But you have lamby.

Riding bikes in the yard.
Fast,
Faster.
You're in front this time.
A scream
So loud it touches the sky.

Make sure she has lamby.

Hospital corridors,
Long and white.

My shoes echo and I run
Fast,
Faster.
To be beside you in your bed.
You have lamby.

The Lost Friend

We both hate PE.
I never noticed you before,
Now it's just you and me.
I throw you a ball,
You break a nail.
Friends.

"I thought you were an emo
Because of your pencil case."
We laugh.
We hate PE.
But I look forward to it now.

A slow transition.
Lunch times with old friends,
Replaced.
Lunches with you,
In science building staircases;
You prefer the outdoors.

A boy on the bus.
A boy the the train.
We walk together on a T day,
We talk about our crushes.
Nothing is more important.

Our minds enveloped by our love.
And yet now
I don't think of that crush.
I think of you
And our friendship lost.

Loving Kindness

Learn from the past.
Plan for the future.
But always remember,
To live in the present.

Be kind.
Be brave.
Be curious.

Kindness;
More powerful than hate.
Equanimity;
More freeing than anger.

A tiny ant,
A human.
Both lives.
Both feel pain.

Stop and listen.
The trickling of water.
The chirping of birds.
Be here.

Tudor Mews

The cats look out the windows,
Sitting on the window ledge.
Looking at the bees
In the flowers.
Red
Yellow
Pink
We like the blue ones best.

An elderly neighbour
Waddles our way.
Says "hello.
Welcome to the Villa."

A lamp post
Blue trimmings
A bird bath
Little trees
Cottage flowers
In the villa at Tudor Mews

Why move to a cottage in England
When you can move to Tudor Mews.

The Beach

Feet on burning sand
Wind blowing in eyes
Seaweed wet and slimy
Water cold
Waves splash in face
Can we go home yet?

childhood summers
Sunscreen
Sand in shoes
Let's stay home and make a movie

Today
Baby toes in sandals
Sunscreen on his little nose
Carried down to the sand
Splash in the waves
Refreshing
He giggles
"Bubbles!"

Trucks in sand
Building moats
Warm sun

Sand catches his fall
He giggles
Can we stay here forever?

Wedding Day

Go to the window,
Check the weather
A fine day for a wedding.

A pretty flower
A photo from childhood
A last goodbye
Bathroom conversations;
All make me almost cry.

Green velvet
Pink flowers
Willow trees
Small details that don't matter.
It's just me and you.

Crash

Look at the sheep
Look at the sea
Look at the beach
Look out.

My chest hurts
My hands are shaking
I check my eye isn't bleeding.

Can I walk?

Cuddles in the garden.
Phone calls to parents:
"I love you."
She never says that.
Today I do.

Gummy worms on the floor.
Windy walks on the sand,
I hold your hand.
We are okay.

Today,
Behind the wheel,
My chest no longer hurts.
And yet my hands are still shaking.

Purple Hutch - 2010

Purple hutch to keep him safe
Purple hutch
Lift the lid
No freedom
No white rabbit
Late
Check his watch
No where to go
Stuck in a hutch
Purple hutch
Colour the entrapment
Colour the pain
Shut the lid
Forever

Train to nowhere - 2010

I stand in the crowd alone.
More alone than when I'm by myself.
I sit on a train going nowhere,
It has a vague sense of purpose.
Less alone with a goal,
Less alone with a purpose.
So I catch the train to nowhere,
Call it somewhere.
It's cool and its calm,
It's empty and it's full.
The train to nowhere is mine.

The love of friends - 2010

Love.
Friendship.
You,
Me.
Us.
Friends.
Love expanded,
Love compressed,
The love between us
Is surely the best.
Friends.

Can't go on - 2010

I can't go on like this
Sitting alone
Sitting at home.
An entire day worth nothing,
No memories,
No real joy.
I miss living,
I miss life,
But most of all
I miss myself.

Fight - 2010

I find a bead of blood beneath my sheets,
A wispy willow and the misty mountain weeps.
Bind my reflection to the shadows of your soul,
A burst of light,
A dove of warmth,
The anger blinds us
And it cannot find us,
Beneath the crispin folds on linen blood.

Velvet Eyes - 2010

Velvet eyes,
Make no compromise.
And the hazel swirls
Of confetti and tears
As the years
Just slip,
Gently burn away.

The End - 2010

I hold your little hand in mine
Take me back
Take me back in time.
Hold your broken weight up to the stars,
And it comes as no surprise
The end is near.
I tell you there is nothing to fear,
But the end is drawing near.
The end is near.

Young and old,
Worn and cold.
The unravelling of what's already been undone.
We cannot stop what is yet to come,
Your fearless fate has already began.
That journey to the centre of the sun.
Young and old,
A thousand memories you hold.
They will live on when your time is done.

Lonely Man - 2010

The day begins with a bang
He gets up
He splashes his face.
And the satin dress looks out of place,
Draped across his chair.
As if it were possessed,
As if it simply didn't belong there.
As he combs his hair,
Clumsily trips on her shoes,
He has nothing
So there was nothing for him to loose.
Now he has a memory,
One dream,
One memory.
A burden for eternity.

One day - 2010

Peppermint seahorse,
Satin blue dream.
One day you will realise,
Things aren't as they seem.

Cornfields and roses,
Spilled milk, empty hope.
One day you will realise,
It's impossible to cope.

Paper ballerina,
Cranberry pie.
One day you will realise,
We all have to die.

Hello - 2011

Stars are sparkling in the sky
A weary astronaut
Bid me goodbye
An eruption of noise
A confliction of sound
A volcano rumbling high in the clouds
Of marshmallow soup
And of dirty clean shoes
Up in the roof a fairy escapes.